Local Wildlife Series : 1

(Series Editor : Tony Soper)

WILDLIFE
OF THE
DART ESTUARY

CW00820288

By the same author

The Bird Table Book
The Wreck of the Torrey Canyon (with Crispin Gill and
    Frank Booker)
Penguins (with John Sparks)
Owls (with John Sparks)
Beachcombing
Wildlife Begins at Home
Everyday Birds
Beside the Sea (with Hilary Soper)
Birdwatch
The National Trust Book of the Coast
Discovering Birds
Discovering Animals

In the same series as this volume:

Wildlife of the Exe estuary: Stan Davies
Wildlife of the Fal estuary: Roger Burrows

Front Cover: The mouth of the Dart, from
Jubilee Path, Dartmouth. *(Eric Wingate)*

WILDLIFE
OF THE
DART ESTUARY

Tony Soper

Line drawings by Robin Prytherch

Maps by Hilary Soper

Series Editor: Tony Soper

Harbour Books : Dartmouth

1986

First published in Great Britain in 1982 by Harbour Books,
12 Fairfax Place, Dartmouth, Devon TQ6 9AE

Second edition 1986

© Tony Soper 1982, 1986

British Library Cataloguing in Publication Data

Soper, Tony
 Wildlife of the Dart Estuary.——2nd ed.——
 (Local wildlife; 1)
 1. Estuarine fauna——England——Dart, River,
 Estuary
 I. Title   II. Series
 591.9423′592   QL256

 ISBN 0-907906-05-2

Photoset in 10/11 point Times

Printed by
Tozer & Co. (Printers) Ltd, Dartmouth

CONTENTS

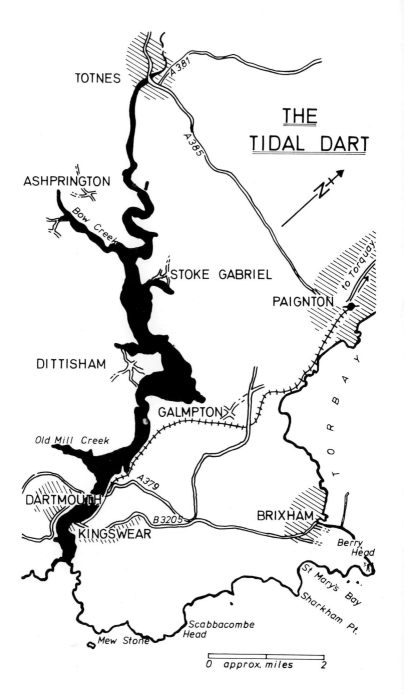

INTRODUCTION

The Dart is the major Dartmoor river, not the longest but the most all-embracing, tumbling down from a maze of tributaries reaching over the high Moor. While the moorland journey is of torrents over a boulder-strewn watercourse, when the Dart reaches the sea it becomes a placid winding thing. Although a south-easterly gale can make even the harbour a lively place for small boats, it has an intimate scale and a warmth which charms away all complaints.

The estuary is commonly known locally as the 'river', and since it lacks the extensive and broad reaches of more shallow estuaries it is difficult not to feel some sympathy for this incorrect usage. But whatever it is called, the tidal Dart is worth seeing, and the best way to explore it is from the deck of a boat. Best of all, start from Dartmouth just after low water, on the beginnings of the flood, and work your way slowly up, skirting the edge of the mudbanks.

From the harbour entrance to the limit of navigation at Totnes, the winding reaches cover just over eleven miles, as the cormorant flies. It can be seen in an hour, if you go straight up the middle and break the speed limit. Better to travel slowly. It is a difficult estuary to sail, with flukey and boisterous winds. Spend a couple of weeks sniffing out the likely places, stick on the mud a few times and wait for the birds to come to you. It is an enjoyable waterway, with more than a touch of genuine wilderness about it.

T.S.
March 1986

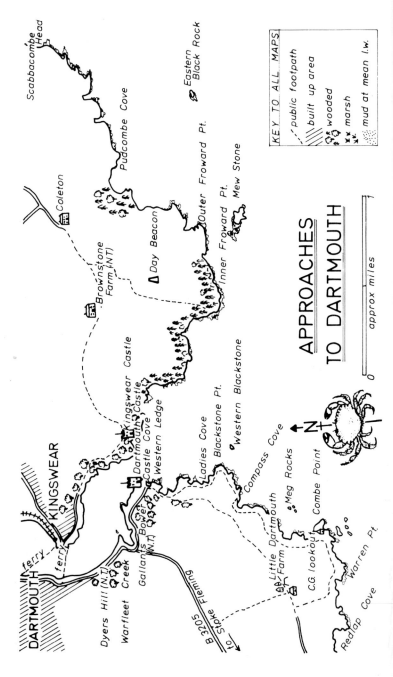

Scabbacombe Head

Pudcombe Cove

Eastern Black Rock

Coleton

Outer Froward Pt.

Brownstone Farm (NT)

△ Day Beacon

Inner Froward Pt.

Mew Stone

KINGSWEAR

Kingswear Castle

Western Blackstone

DARTMOUTH

Dartmouth Castle

Castle Cove

Western Ledge

Blackstone Pt.

Ladies Cove

ferry

ferry

Dyers Hill (N.T)

Warfleet Creek

Gallants Bower (N.T)

Compass Cove

Meg Rocks

Little Dartmouth Farm

Combe Point

B 3205 Fleming

to Stoke

C.G. lookout

Warren Pt.

Redlap Cove

N

KEY TO ALL MAPS

— — — public footpath

///// built up area

🌲🌲 wooded

marsh

mud at mean l.w.

APPROACHES TO DARTMOUTH

0   approx miles   1

8

I

APPROACHES TO DARTMOUTH

Sailing up Channel from the west, after rounding Start Point, the entrance to Dartmouth is well marked by a conspicuous beacon. Perched some 500 feet above Froward Point it is an 80-foot high pyramidal Day Mark of limestone. Approaching down Channel from the east (or coming out of Torbay in a pleasure steamer), your first conspicuous mark is the limestone mass of **Berry Head** looming up on the far side of Lyme Bay.

Berry Head is home for a community of wild plants and, in the summer, for breeding colonies of kittiwakes and guillemots, some four hundred pairs of each. There are also a number of fulmars, jackdaws and feral pigeons. The guillemots have taken over the horizontal ledges just left of the cave which is a sea-level feature of the first promontory south-west of the lighthouse head. The kittiwakes, as well as filling the cave with raucous calls, have spread rather more widely over the vertical cliff faces. Some herring gull nests are perched on the less dramatic cliff slopes, but most of them enjoy the safety of the several islands just offshore.

A few shags breed here, too. From the end of July there is a good chance of seeing purple sandpipers on the rocky ledges at the edge of the sea, as well as parties of turnstones. The first arrivals will still be wearing their bright breeding plumage. Although the sandpiper is not exactly a colourful bird, its dull yellow legs set off the portly shape of its dark body and it has a certain presence which makes it attractive. Both the sandpiper and the turnstones are tame, confiding birds, dodging about amongst the seaweedy rocks, but they may be surprisingly difficult to see till you get your eye in. The most likely spots are the Mew Stone and Cod Rock islands.

Working close inshore, the next birdy place is the rocky

(Simon McBride)

The cliff ledges of Berry Head are home for a multitude of seabirds.

escarpment on the northern side of **St. Mary's Bay**. Again there is a chance of turnstones and purple sandpipers, possibly oystercatchers, at the water's edge, but, higher up, there is a flourishing colony of feral pigeons. These are mostly racing pigeons which have opted out of the race, usually on passage from their release point in France and on their way back home to the Midlands. Having successfully crossed the Channel, they find a sympathetic resting place on the cliff tops and plenty of suitable nesting crevices and they take to a hippy life style, spending a certain amount of time at the Torbay beaches and car parks cadging food. But their ancestral breeding stock was the wild coastal rock dove, sadly now extinct in these parts, and they soon feel very much at home flying about these wild bays and giving spectacular aerobatic displays.

Farther offshore there is always the chance of a party of fishing gannets. Their nearest breeding place is off Alderney in the Channel Islands, but they think nothing of the sixty mile passage to South Devon for the better fishing. Mostly you can see them circling and plunge-diving for mackerel, but on occasion they may be swimming on the surface. Flocks of anything up to a few dozen common scoters are not uncommon offshore. They are non-breeding birds which occur irregularly,

Top left: Great skua. Top right: Adult and juvenile gannet. Below: Common scoters.

but may be plentiful in some summers. The sea-going ducks tend to sit on the water in compact parties, the drakes have a glossy black plumage, but you will be lucky to get close enough to see the marked yellow patch on the black bill.

Puffins are most conspicuous by their absence in these parts, sadly. Earlier in the century they bred at Berry Head, but, as at so many of their southern stations, they have long since withdrawn. However, we not infrequently see single ones well out to sea, two or three miles offshore, just paddling along and minding their own business.

On a day of glassy calm, you will often see jellyfish pulsating through the surface waters. The commonest will be *Aurelia*, some 6–8 inches across, with its four purple rings. A larger—and stinging—animal is *Chrysaora*, milky-white with a central brown spot and radial brown streaks. Then there is *Rhizostoma*, the biggest, up to two feet across and quite harmless; it is pale green or blue, with a darker purple fringe. You will be lucky indeed to see the sail of *Velella*, 'Jack-by-the-wind', a jellyfish which has a hard ridge 'sail' which extends right across its diameter; and equally lucky to see the air-filled bladder of a Portuguese Man-o-War jellyfish. Both of these are driven about the oceans by winds as well as currents, unlike our more familiar jellyfish which swim just below the surface using a jet-propulsion system.

Calm days in June are also the most likely to reveal basking sharks, although they are not at all common east of Start Point. Cruising about slowly, just under the surface as they strain vast quantities of sea water for its plankton, the tip of the snout, dorsal and tail fins show clear of the water. They are quite harmless—unless you collide with them when you are in danger from the violence of their lashing tail as they dive.

The cliffs just inside **Scabbacombe Head** support a flourishing sea bird community. The two hundred or so kittiwake pairs will be obvious enough, to say nothing of their noise. There are also more than forty pairs of fulmars breeding here, nesting on

Left: Auks on a rocky ledge, with close-up of razorbill (left) and guillemot. Right, above: Raven. Below: Fulmar.

ledges just below the vegetation line along the top of the cliff. Tucked away rather inconspicuously amongst the kittiwakes there are a dozen or two guillemots with sometimes a pair or two of razorbills. They have chosen a horizontal ledge rather more than half-way up the cliff, in the middle of the main seabird area. One of the very few oystercatcher pairs to breed in South Devon patronise a ledge not far away. There may also be sandpipers and turnstones feeding near the water line.

Throughout the summer one of the most attractive things about Scabbacombe Bay is the socialising parties of kittiwakes and fulmars which usually take place a couple of hundred yards from the shore. Off Scabbacombe Head there may be several dozen fulmars engaged in courtship water-dances. Black guillemots are vagrants to Devon but we had the luck to see one in July 1979 swimming about at just this place, so it is worth keeping your eyes open. But generally speaking the commonest auks here are guillemots, with razorbills a poor second, and puffins few and far between.

From July to September there are a fair number of terns about, post-breeding or non-breeding birds since no terns breed in Devon. Sandwich terns are not uncommon along this coast, while black terns are very much less common. Both may be seen fishing, but the most likely sighting is of sandwich terns perching

Sandwich tern.

(Jan van de Kam)

on an offshore rock, for instance the **Druid's Mare**, at low water. These are all passage birds, on their way to winter in West Africa.

Our inshore waters support a vast population of seabirds, sustained by the fish and plankton-rich waters supplied by the North Atlantic Current which springs from the Caribbean and the Gulf Stream. The seafaring life of birds may be hard, but it is relatively safe. With few predators about and plenty of food they tend to be long-lived. Of the dozen families, such as gulls, terns, petrels, auks and gannets, few are truly pelagic, mostly they are coastal foragers. Most are carnivorous, though some of the gulls are omnivorous. Although their food comes directly from the sea, in the shape of a variety of fish and invertebrates, they live in harmony by virtue of their varying food targets and their different methods of fishing.

Reaching along towards Dartmouth, the next bird-stop is the **Mewstone**, a striking pinnacle of slate with a thin crust of soil round its lower slopes. There are plenty of ledges and crevices which, allied to a marked lack of interference by people, encourages a thriving breeding place for coastal birds. The main nesting area is on the north side, away from exposure to the open sea. Herring gulls, and a few great blackbacks, half-a-dozen or more pairs of shags and a couple of dozen pairs of cormorants live here in tolerant community. With local knowledge it is possible to edge in very close without disturbing them. While the cormorants have established a loosely-knit colony stretching over the top of the island, the shags prefer a certain isolation, and darker crevices nearer the sea. Superficially similar birds, they share similar habits and nesting

The Dartmouth Mewstone, home for breeding seabirds.

(Tony Soper)

Centre: Adult cormorant in post-breeding plumage. Other birds clockwise from bottom left: Juvenile shag, adult shag in post-breeding plumage, adult shag in breeding plumage, adult cormorant in breeding plumage, juvenile cormorant.

preferences and their fishing territories overlap to some extent. But outside the breeding season the cormorants are birds of the river and muddy estuary, while shags rarely show their faces on fresh or estuary water though they may sometimes come inside the harbour in particularly bad weather. The cormorants are larger birds, sporting a white face and throat patch in breeding plumage, as well as a striking white patch at the side below the wings. Shags lack the white trim and carry a crest at breeding time. Immatures of both species have off-white shirt fronts, but the young cormorants are markedly whiter.

At low water there is an extensive spread of rocky ledges on the west side of the Mewstone. Gulls roost and feed here, and it is a favourite hauling-out place for grey seals. South Devon has only one breeding station for this species, and this is a good deal further west, but individuals are not uncommon along this coast at any time of year. On the Mewstone, in summer, if you choose the right time—low water of spring tides—you have a fair chance of seeing one. On one memorable June day in 1976, there were actually three cow grey seals sunning themselves at the water's edge. We have also watched them fishing close in, and on another memorable day saw a massive bull holding a large ray in both fore-flippers as he tore its flesh apart. In times past, the people of the south-west regarded seal meat as a welcome addition to a feast but mostly seals were hunted for their skins and blubber.

Eider ducks sometimes show up at the Mewstone. Although they are most frequent in winter, there are many records of summering, non-breeders. Great skuas are regular passers-by, mostly as single birds. Although superficially confused with the more-or-less brown juvenile gulls, their demeanour is unmistakably hawkish. Like gulls, they are scavengers, but as pirates they are aggressive in chasing terns and forcing them to give up their catch. Manx shearwaters on passage converge as they pass Start Point later in the summer, in September/October, and you may see small numbers close inshore off Dartmouth, especially in foggy conditions.

Like the smaller Mewstone of Berry Head, the Dartmouth Mewstone is good for purple sandpipers and turnstones. We once saw a turnstone being taken by a sparrowhawk here. The slope of the Mewstone is steep and the hawk had quite a struggle to get off the ground with its prey, its wings beating against the rocks as it forced itself up into the air, the wader still fluttering helplessly in its claws. We don't often see sparrowhawks in such a maritime environment, but this whole coastline is prime country for buzzards and ravens. Peregrines are decidedly uncommon, but regular. Keep an eye out for them at the seabird cliffs and wherever the feral pigeons congregate. On one fine August day we saw two ravens, a buzzard and a kestrel all in the air together above the coast just inshore of the Mewstone. On the surface of the water there will often be herring gulls and great blackbacks, kittiwakes (especially at the end of the breeding season) and on most days you should see several auks. From August onwards there will be father-and-child pairs of razorbills paddling about just offshore, the juvenile following obediently just behind its parent.

The Mewstone will have been a useful pilotage mark when approaching from the east. Keep a good lookout for crab-pot markers, for the riser lines can be a menace to small boats. Sometimes the pots are well marked with flagged dan-buoys, but equally often they are attached to empty polythene flasks which are not easy to see. Several awkward rocks reveal themselves only at low water up to three cables W.S.W. of the Mewstone, so it is as well to keep the Eastern Black Rock well open after passing, before making for the conical buoy of Castle Ledge. Tidal currents are weak in the offing, but in the entrance they may reach nearly four knots on the ebb at springs, especially if there has been a lot of rain. The entrance is easy enough under power but the high land on either side produces wayward squalls which are a test for anyone under sail. But, on the bright side, there is no bar and the harbour is open at all times.

Along the cliff slopes of **Inner Froward Point** there is an impressive shelter belt of Monterey Pines, with their bright emerald-green needles. Elsewhere in the world these fast-growing trees are important commercially, but their rather coarse timber has little money value in Britain. They are salt-tolerant and gale-resistant so they provide us with shelter belts on exposed parts of the coast which might otherwise be treeless.

Kingswear Castle protects the eastern side of the harbour entrance. Nowadays it functions as a private home, and the gentle rocky ledges below it are used by gulls as a roosting place. There may be the odd oystercatcher and it is a favoured visiting place for whimbrels on autumn passage.

On the opposite side of the entrance you come first to **Ladies Cove**, just inside the **Western Blackstone**. A few dozen herring gulls and a handful of shags have their nests here. It is possible to venture in quite close, but take good care of the large number of crab store-pots and their attendant lines and marker floats.

At **Castle Cove**, just inside the Western Ledge, there is

another herring gullery, and this is a place where you may invariably see the gulls roosting on the branches of the oaks in somewhat untypical fashion. (Lesser black-backed gulls are not common, perhaps half-a-dozen pairs breed on the cliff slopes at Stoke Fleming, a couple of miles further west).

Dartmouth Castle was first built in the late fourteenth century, to provide a 'stronge and myghtye defensyve tower'. The piratical operations of the Dartmouth men had invited reprisal, so there was a powerful reason for guarding the entrance and Custom House income provided the funds. The present building was completed during the period 1481–94, about the same time as Kingswear Castle. A chain was forged to stretch across the narrow entrance, reaching to the Gommerock blockhouse on the opposite side, and this was raised into position at night. Dartmouth Castle is grouped, to great scenic effect, with the seventeenth century church of **St. Petrox.**

Once inside the strong currents of the entrance, you find yourself in a superb, sheltered, deep-water anchorage. Intimate in scale and generally tranquil in atmosphere, the deep water is almost entirely land-locked. There is plenty of room for a large number of vessels and it is no surprise that the harbour has been

Dartmouth Castle (Kingswear Castle on the opposite side of the entrance).

(Reg Green)

important since the early Middle Ages. Its maritime history dates back to the Crusades. From the twelfth till the fifteenth centuries it supported a profitable wine trade with Bordeaux, along with the equally profitable piracy and merchant adventuring of the times. Towards the end of the sixteenth century the Newfoundland cod fishery replaced piracy. Cargoes of salt fish were carried to Spain and Portugal, return journeys with wines made the Dartmouth families rich. Dartmouth remained an important port till after Elizabethan times, but, as the fortunes of Plymouth increased, it declined to its present happy state.

Dartmouth itself is a welcoming town of steep streets, narrow passages and endless flights of steps. While the town now presents a comfortable jumble of architectural styles, shapes, sizes and colours, it has grown around a central core which still offers some splendid half-timbered, overhung and gabled houses of the fifteenth and sixteenth centuries. In fact, the earliest settlements were on the high ground well back from the existing waterfront, but infilling of what must have been a bird-rich creek has provided land for what is now the main shopping area. Higher Street, the Butterwalk and Bayard's Cove with its cobbled Quay, provide the evidence of great wealth in the past. Nowadays they echo in summer to the screaming fly-pasts of a healthy population of swifts. Apart from these 'devil-birds' the town does not offer much to the birdwatcher, though the Boat Float will have its complement of begging gulls and mute swans attending the endless generosity of both residents and visitors. In the elms of the Royal Avenue Gardens a small rookery has its off-years and its on-years. A fair number of herring gulls breed on hospitable roof-tops, as they commonly do nowadays in West Country resorts and fishing ports. Probably the best place to see cormorants fishing, sometimes at remarkably close quarters, is off the **South Embankment.**

Dartmouth is linked to the village of **Kingswear** by two ferries. There is a passenger service, now run privately, which was originally set up by the railway company when steam trains arrived in 1864—but on the 'wrong' side of the river. Dartmouth 'station' must surely have been the only railway station in England without an inch of rail to be seen. And there is the Lower Ferry, run by the Local Authority, a very much more ancient service offering a salutary lesson to anyone who enjoys seeing boat-handling at its best. A car-carrying float is tended by a tug which operates a side-by-side tow. The operating skills which shunt the float to-and-fro in ever-changing conditions of wind, current and traffic are marvellous to see. In late summer, as the ramp of the ferry is lowered, just as the float approaches the hard, it may scoop bucketfuls of silver whitebait from the sea, an astonishing sight.

Kingswear is the base for the Dartmouth crabbing fleet. More crabs are landed here than at any other port in the country. The sturdy fishing vessels work well out to sea, perhaps twenty or thirty miles, tending their strings of pots every day the weather allows. They may have a dozen strings of forty pots each, representing a total value of some £10,000, an investment which spends most of its time sitting on the sea-bed, highly vulnerable to passing trawls and foul weather. But, if they are lucky, the fishermen may bring a couple of dozen tea chests full of crabs back to Kingswear. Most of these crabs are hens, the proportion of hens to cocks is something like twenty to one. Naturally enough the crabbers wonder how long the bonanza will continue. In 1972, 1340 tonnes of crabs were landed at Kingswear, with a value of £154,800. In 1980, 2241 tonnes fetched £1,144,817. Both edible and spider crabs fetch a ready market on the Continent, served by refrigerated trailers which cross to Roscoff from Plymouth by Brittany Ferries.

Crabbers at Kingswear.

(Tony Soper)

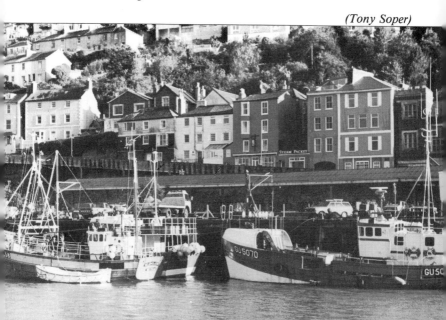

II

THE LOWER REACHES

Dartmouth Harbour is dominated by the massive but uninspiring **Britannia Royal Naval College** (1899–1905). But it is easy to imagine the noble view enjoyed by the succession of fortunate midshipmen. Before it was shore-based, the college operated from hulks moored in the river. Nowadays there are no accommodation-hulks, but the peaceful anchorage is well-filled with vessels of all kinds. There may be timber ships waiting for a fair tide to Totnes, Eastern-bloc stern-trawlers buying-in horse mackerel, naval minesweepers, patrol vessels, submarines and, surpassing all in numbers if not always in elegance, the pleasure yachts and motor boats.

Be sure to cast a quick glance over the mooring buoys, because they provide safe and undisturbed roosting places for gulls, terns, cormorants and even waders. Black-headed gulls roost at night on the boats moored close in to the **North Embankment** from the end of June. They do not breed in Devon, but come here in vast numbers as soon as they can decently leave their breeding areas. Herons may roost on these boats at night, indeed they will even fish at night in the waters of the Marinas, where fish are attracted by the bright arc-lights. Even grey seals enjoy the harbourside lights, especially in winter, when they come up after bass.

The railway embankment on the Kingswear side of the estuary provides a copybook example of the zonation of seaweeds, although it lacks the deepwater kelps as it is rooted in mud at low water. When the tide is in, grey mullet graze on the algae both on the embankment and on the bottoms of the boats. Boats left afloat here soon develop a fringe of green weed round the waterline and this attracts the mullet. On a calm day you can quite literally hear them smacking their lips as they munch the fresh greenery. Although they breed at sea, grey mullet feed

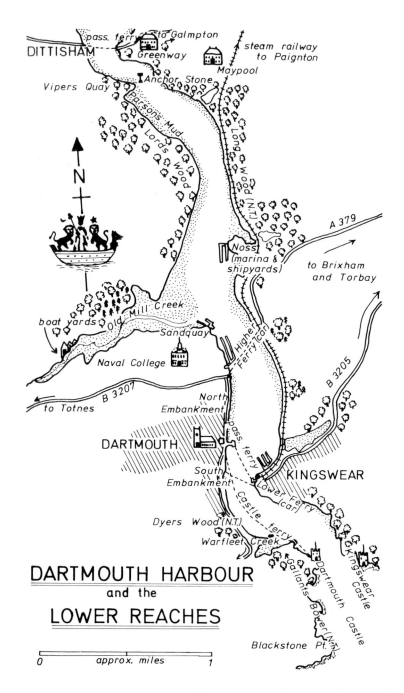

pass. ferry to Galmpton
DITTISHAM
Greenway
steam railway to Paignton
Maypool
Anchor Stone
Vipers Quay
Parsons Mud
Lords Wood
Long Wood (N.T.)
A 379
N
Noss (marina & shipyards)
to Brixham and Torbay
Mill Creek
boat yards
Old
Sandquay
Higher Ferry (car)
Naval College
B 3205
to Totnes
B 3207
North Embankment
DARTMOUTH
pass. ferry
KINGSWEAR
South Embankment
Lower Ferry (car)
Dyers Wood (N.T.)
Castle ferry
Warfleet Creek
Gallants Bower (N.T.)
Dartmouth Castle
Kingswear Castle

DARTMOUTH HARBOUR
and the
LOWER REACHES

0   approx. miles   1

mainly in the muddy water of estuaries. Lacking teeth, they browse on seaweeds and strain food from the mud using the fine comb-like fringes on their lips. Flounders also spawn at sea, but· they are the only flatfish to patronise an estuary, tolerating the fresher water for months on end. Their prey is cockles and other shells, shore crabs and shrimps, and in turn they are preyed on by fishermen and fisherbirds like the cormorant. At one time pilchards sometimes came into the lower reaches in vast numbers, but no more.

The diesel-electric Higher Ferry paddle-wheels its way across wire cables from Sandquay, by the Dart Marina, to Noss, linking Dartmouth with Brixham and Torbay. Especially at night, gulls, and occasionally, herons, may perch on its ramps. The ferry was built by Philip & Son Ltd, who not so long ago maintained a flourishing boatyard where their marina lies, but who have now retreated to their main shipyard at Noss.

Top left: Common gull. Top right: Great black-backed gull. Below left: Black-headed gull in winter and (behind) summer plumage. Lower right: Adult herring gull, first summer and first winter juveniles.

Although not active in building nowadays (they built in steel; landing craft in the last war, and more recently, Chay Blyth's 'British Steel') they do a fair amount of repair work. There may be a coaster or a Brixham trawler or two on or lying off their building slips. Just before you reach the **Noss Marina** there is a small bay with the rotting wreck of a fishing boat hull lying in its mud. This is a fairly good place for waders like redshanks.

On the opposite side of the river lies the open entrance to **Old Mill Creek**, with serried ranks of small naval craft on mooring trots across it. From July into September this is a favourite place for common and arctic terns and, much less frequently, black terns. At low water the extensive mud bank supports quite a few oystercatchers, herons, gulls and crows.

When the mudflats cover, the birds may roost on one of the Navy's pontoons, or on the gunwhales of the wreck of an Irish sailing coaster, the 'Invermore' of Castleford, which lies stuck fast in the middle of the mudbank.

Terns prefer to perch on the mooring buoys, or, sometimes, on the truck of a yacht's masthead. Common terns, distinguished with some difficulty from the arctic terns by the black tip to the orangey-red bill, breed mainly on the east coast but are passage birds here on their way to winter in South Africa. The arctic terns, breeding not surprisingly in the Arctic, are long-

Gulls crowding the gunwhales of the derelict 'Invermore'.

(Tony Soper)

Top: Sandwich tern in summer plumage. On middle buoy: Black tern in winter plumage. Lower buoy: Common tern. In flight, top: Black tern in summer plumage and arctic tern. Bottom: Common tern.

distance travellers, passing through on their way to winter in Antarctica, by way of the coast of West Africa, a journey of some 10,000 miles.

Scan the shoreline for herons as the banks of the estuary close in slightly above Noss, to enclose a deep-water reach (6 fathoms) capable of sheltering thousands of tons of laid-up shipping. The shores rise steeply, thickly wooded with oaks. **Long Wood**, on the east side, now belongs to the National Trust. Its timber was once exploited for shipbuilding and for charcoal. The requirement for ship's frames was for trunks or branches of great strength, growing in open plan, with room to develop massive branches low down on the bole. The shipwright would search for the right shape in the growing timber before cutting it. Charcoal burners were less selective, requiring only a limitless supply of small stuff. Their product was used for metal smelting and in the glass industry.

The deep water continues on the east side of the reach, while there is a moderately interesting patch of mud on the west side, **Parson's Mud.** If you are very lucky, you might see a mink running along the foreshore at the back of the mud, but there is a great deal less likelihood of an otter. Apart from the fact that they are largely nocturnal, they are thin on the ground even in this county, one of their ancestral strongholds. Fortunately there are some parts of South Devon where they are holding their own. Some people have blamed the success of the introduced mink for their decline, but there seems little evidence of this.

At least the mink show themselves by day, indeed it is characteristic of them that they treat people with something approaching indifference, if not disdain. Often mistaken for otters, their faces are less broad and they are smaller. Although they have been regarded as a serious pest, attacking domestic fowls and waterfowl, it seems likely that this nuisance has been over-rated, and without much doubt we must learn to live with them. They are easy enough to spot. Ferret-sized and dark chocolate brown, they have tails as bushy as a cat. They swim and dive freely.

There may be a heron or two fishing at the edge of Parson's Mud, and maybe up to a dozen roosting on the dark and undisturbed foreshore and low tree branches. Their birthplace is on the opposite bank, between **Maypool** and **Greenway**, but this is best seen from the west side because the heronry is almost concealed in the canopies of a stand of Scots Pines. Look left a couple of hundred yards from Maypool boathouse and then high up in the trees close to the water's edge. Right through the

Herons breed in tall Scots Pines at Maypool. Above: Adult and juveniles. Below: Juvenile and adult fishing.

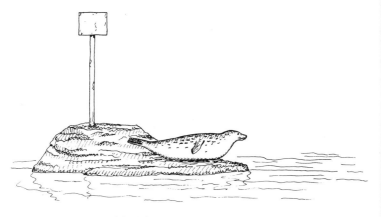

A cow grey seal basking on the Anchor Stone at half-tide.

spring and summer months there will be birds standing close to the nests or on the bulky nests themselves. As the summer progresses the young birds become more and more visible. One of our jobs is to perform the annual count of herons for the British Trust for Ornithology and in 1981, for instance, there were ten nests here. This represents a small decline in numbers, probably the result of some inevitable disturbance caused by tree-felling operations. As we shall see, the displaced birds have set up embryonic heronries higher up the estuary. At least, nowadays, they are welcomed almost anywhere, a far cry from times as recent as the last century when they were regarded with universal hostility.

The heronry is established in the grounds of the Greenway Estate. Greenway House is now owned by relatives of the late Dame Agatha Christie but, for centuries, it was the home of the Gilbert family. Step-brothers to Sir Walter Raleigh, Humphrey and Adrian Gilbert were also Elizabethan seaman-explorers of great renown. It was Sir Humphrey who claimed Newfoundland for the Queen in 1583, spawning the highly profitable fishing for cod off the Newfoundland Banks. The Gilbert family were also involved in the search for the legendary North-West Passage.

The channel continues to run deep on the Greenway side, and past Greenway boathouse it expands into a bay. Scan the overhanging branches, close to the water, for kingfishers; this seems to be a favourite place for them. The Dart is well stocked with kingfishers, especially in the last half of the year and in deep winter, when families which started life higher up in the fresh water find their way down to the salt.

The banks close in to create a bottle-neck around the **Anchor Stone**, a hazardous rock which rears out of the depths to lie in wait for unwary sailors. The currents run hard here, and on occasion the rock, with its day-mark, looks as if it is steaming along at a rate of knots. For the last couple of years it has become a hauling-out place for the occasional grey seal, basking in the sun and the appreciation of passing tourists.

Kingfisher

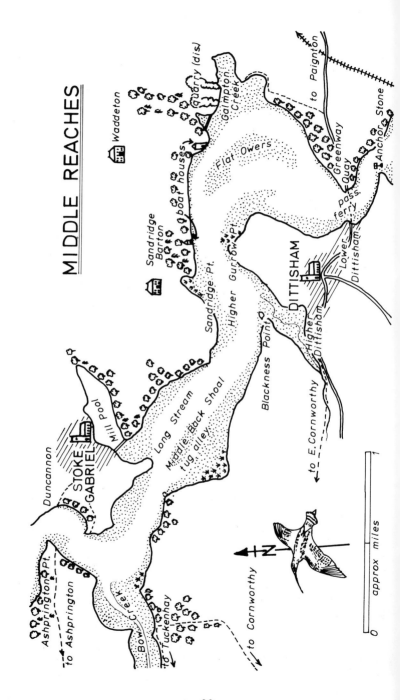

MIDDLE REACHES

to Paignton

Anchor Stone

Greenway Quay

Waddeton

Quarry (dis.)

Galmpton Creek

pass. ferry

Flat Owers

boat houses

Sandridge Barton

Lower Dittisham

Sandridge Pt.

Higher Gurrow Pt.

DITTISHAM

Long Stream

Middle Back Shoal tug alley

Blackness Point

Higher Dittisham

Duncannon

Mill Pool

STOKE GABRIEL

to E. Cornworthy

Ashprington Pt.

to Ashprington

Bow Creek

to Tuckenhay

to Cornworthy

N

0   approx miles   1

III

THE MIDDLE REACHES

Once past the Anchor Stone the estuary begins to open out. From **Greenway Quay** on the east side a passenger ferry crosses to the village of **Dittisham**, a dense straggle of cottages comfortably sheltered by the steep rise of the hills. Not so long ago the fertile fields hereabouts grew prodigious quantities of damsons. At high water we are now faced with a great expanse of open estuary. At low water of spring tides, this is the lower end of a three-mile stretch which is biologically the most interesting on the Dart.

The Dart's estuary is in fact a drowned valley, a 'ria', in the classic geological style. Its mud and sandbanks are the result of a large-scale deposition of silt which began with the end of the last glaciation. Before the Pleistocene Ice Age the Dart had carved its preferred route to the sea, but when the ice was formed vast quantities of water were stored, frozen, up on the land, so that the sea level dropped by as much as 60 metres. Because the gradient from the land to the sea was now so much steeper, the river flowed faster and with increased energy, so that deep gorge-like valleys were excavated. When the ice melted, the sea-level rose again, allowing the salt water to return and drown the over-deepened lower reaches and river mouth.

The return of the sea meant that the river slowed down again and, as a result, more and more sediment was deposited. So much sediment, in fact, that the rias became filled with sediment won from the land. The mudbanks may be tens of metres deep, and the sedimentation continues, all the processes of deposition striving to raise the shimmering mud to the status of dry land. But, barring reclamation schemes, it will be a very long time before we are deprived of these bird-rich tidal mudbanks.

A bold promontory above Dittisham throws the course of the river well over to the east side in a great curve. At low water it

31

will be necessary for most boats to take the deepwater channel which lies close in to the wooded east shore. This suits the birdwatcher very well becaue it is the best way to scan the gritty surface of **Flat Owers**, a mighty tidal bank which actually scrapes the bottoms of many unwary yachts. There will often be men busy digging bait with garden forks and filling buckets with ragworms and lugworms and, because Flat Owers is worm rich, there are always a fair number of birds about. Apart from the opportunist crows and gulls, there will be curlews and oyster-catchers working the exposed surface, and herons fishing the shallow edge-water.

Galmpton Creek lies on the other side of the channel. Once the boatyards at the head of the creek were famous for con-structing stout wooden fishing vessels for the trawlermen of Brixham. The mud here is sometimes alive with a multitude of black-headed and herring gulls, with a fair scattering of waders.

The rather broken country on the north side of the creek is the remains of a substantial limestone quarry which has been largely rehabilitated in a delightful way by the dense foliage of a wild mixture of ground cover and trees. But there is still plenty of fossil evidence here of earlier days when the area was inundated by a warm coralline sea. Now the channel brings us close in to **Waddeton** boathouse, the ground floor of which houses the cleansing-tanks of Dart Oyster Fisheries. If the tide is well out you may just see the fine mesh trays of Pacific oysters at the

Young herring gull with shore crab. And a curlew.'   *(Jan van de Kam)*

Brixham sailing trawler '*Vigilance*' in Dartmouth harbour.

water's edge, but most oyster activity takes place underwater and out of sight when the growing molluscs filter-feed from the endless flow of plankton and nutrient-rich water passing by.

The oysters are bought in as spat, just a few months old, but within two years they grow to some three to three and a half inches (75–120 grams in weight), the most marketable size. Most go to Birmingham but, of course, many local restaurants are proud to serve them. The oysterman's launch (inevitably called Oystercatcher!) may be in operation, when you will see the trawl hauled in with a harvest of native oysters dredged from the deep channel. The 'natives' do not breed well here, so, again, young specimens about two years old, above 'ring-size', are bought in from the Fal Estuary in Cornwall, to fatten. They face some competition for living space and a lot of predation. Slipper limpets crowd the oysters by taking up too much space, oyster drills bore into them and shore crabs crush them.

These are rich waters and they support unimaginable quantities of life. Apart from the mud-worms, there are many species of shellfish living not only in the mud but on, around and under the salty foreshore. Whelks and winkles, cockles and mussels all find a home here and they are systematically hunted by the fish, when the tide is in, and the birds when the tide is out.

Oystercatchers in flight and feeding. Left: Adult winter. Centre: Adult summer. Right: Juvenile.

Oystercatchers are often working here, although they are not so much looking for oysters as cockles and mussels. With their powerful jemmy of a bill they drive between the two valves of the shellfish and twist them apart to get at the meat. Or, on occasion, they may simply batter the shell and smash it open by direct assault. The other waders, like curlews, find most of their prey by more delicate methods which suit their more delicate bills. The long billed curlews are able to probe gently nearly six inches down into the mud, feeling for their prey with the sensory organs at their bill tips. Yet I have watched them working diligently over the weedy foreshore looking for tougher prey. Head down, and slightly sideways, the bill probes under stones and extracts the yellowy-green shore crabs, eating them whole if they are small. Faced by a big one, say three inches across, they will first pick off the legs one by one and swallow them, then toy with the body for a while before swallowing it whole.

Turnstones are not uncommon here, in small parties. Their stout little bills serve for heavy-duty turning of stones and

Curlew in flight. Below, left: Two curlews. Right: Whimbrel.

weeds, picking off the small fry as it scuttles for cover in the dark weeds. With their mottled tortoiseshell upper parts and short orange legs they are astonishingly well camouflaged and they may be present in fair numbers without anyone being aware of it, until they rise and fly off low over the water, showing a bold pied pattern.

The extensive hards and piling on the foreshore at Waddeton are the remnants of great wartime activity when the U.S. Army prepared here for the invasion of France. Today it is all peaceful enough and the piles serve a useful purpose in that they provide a safe and undisturbed roosting place for cormorants.

The wooded foreshore between here and **Sandridge boathouse** is likely country for herons. Since 1980 there has been some nesting activity in the Scots pines at the water's edge, and it may well be that the decline of the Maypool heronry is in process of encouraging the build-up of nests here, but, so far, there have only been a couple of nests each year. Scan likely-looking dead branches which provide comfortable perches for off-duty herons.

The heron is a sociable bird except when he goes fishing, when he prefers to hunt solo. Each individual has a feeding area which he regards as his own, and he patrols the water's edge as the turning tide brings fish fry and flounders within his reach. While he may spend a good deal of time standing at the water's edge, relaxed, with half an eye open, or standing with outstretched neck, leaning forward to wait for the fish to come to him, his most successful fishing, by far, is accomplished when he stalks actively. Wading very slowly through the shallow water he watches, and then stabs. Small fish are swallowed whole, on the spot. Larger ones are carried off to the nearest field or to the saltings, shaken and broken, then eaten at leisure. As the tide rises over the mudflats, the heron will fly majestically to join his mates, perhaps in a convenient waterside tree, or standing in a group in the middle of an undisturbed field, to preen and rest.

In the summer months salmon netsmen may be working their seines on the well-cleared beach just below Sandbridge boat-house, but the prime seine-netting area is higher up. Keep a watch for buzzards in the Sandridge area. In spring there may be a dozen of them wheeling and mewing as they soar over the tree-fringed fields. There is no shortage of rabbits here, supporting probably a pair of the hawks in every square mile.

Sandridge House was built by John Nash in 1805 but it is on the site of an earlier house in which John Davis was born. The

Redshank.   *(Jan van de Kam)*

Top: Ringed plover. Below left: Dunlin. Right: Turnstone.

first of the great Elizabethan explorers of the Arctic, he was a master navigator whose name is mainly remembered in connection with his search for the North-West Passage which it was hoped would provide a trade route to China and the East by way of Greenland and North America. The Davis Straits were named after him.

Now the channel crosses to the west side of the estuary, towards **Higher Gurrow Point.** The mud between the two Gurrow Points is fairly good for mixed waders, curlews, redshanks, oystercatchers, as well as gulls, herons and cormorants. It is also the most likely place to see ringed plovers, the small stoutly-built waders with the black necklace and black and white head markings. We frequently see anything up to a couple of dozen of them here, usually midway between the water and the shore, and comfortably inside the sandspit which extends out from Higher Gurrow Point. Why they choose this particular place is always something of a mystery, to me anyway.

Long Stream, from the north. The right-hand line of boats marks 'tug alley'. *(Tony Soper)*

As the tide rises the sandspit may be patronised by mixed parties of birds. And when the mud is quite covered many of them will fly the short distance back to the large grass field nearby.

Dittisham Mill Creek now extends back a short distance to the lower parts of the village of **Higher Dittisham.** Dittisham is a two-part village. We passed Lower Dittisham well over a mile downstream, but the configuration of the land has concealed the rather straggly joining of the two halves. If you are now well and truly confused it may be best to look at the map.

Blackness Rock is usually disappointing from a bird point of view. It may be a focal point for a few pairs of half-tame mallards or the odd wader. At high water it is completely under water and yet another small boat hazard. But this is the time when the big grass fields behind it may be a roosting place for large numbers of plovers, curlews and gulls.

We are now comfortably into the longest open reach on the Dart, **Long Stream**. The pleasure steamers all proceed prudently across to the east side by way of Pighole Point (if the tide is in they may well have had enough water to get over Cross Back and deprive you of seeing Higher Gurrow Point but, in exchange, you will sail close to **Sandridge Point** which can be good for turnstones and redshanks) and take you up the main channel past Great Wood and the entrance to Stoke Gabriel Creek. **Stoke Gabriel** village is charming but, from the water, it reveals itself only as a scattering of unattractive bungalows and ill-planned development. But you can just seen the church, which has a huge yew tree in its yard, said to be 1500 years old, which must surely be exaggerated by perhaps 500. The village was once a centre for plum and damson orchards.

Following the main channel is good sense from a pilotage point of view because there is a fearsome shoal—**Middle Back**—extending right down the middle of Long Stream. However, there is a perfectly passable secondary channel on the west side, and if the tide serves and you can persuade the skipper, this passes the most bird-rich mudbanks on the whole of the Dart. There is just enough water for a vessel of three feet draft to get through two and a quarter hours after low water (although the present trend is for it to be silting up) and this is the best possible time to tackle what the Harbour Authority call **'tug alley'**. Work up dead slow between the lines of moored small craft, leave the last trot of boats to starboard (just) and you ought to emerge, flushed and triumphant, at **White Rock**, where you rejoin the main channel. If you stick fast, time will solve your problem and on your way through you will have seen a fine range of waders at close quarters without disturbing them in the least.

Dunlin hunt small shells close to the surface. *(Jan van de Kam)*

The middle section of an estuary is usually wide and expansive, tranquil at first sight yet bursting with life. This west side of Long Stream fits that description well. The wide expanse of mud is bursting with invertebrates which, in turn, support a wide variety of birds and fish. The diversity of birds is possible because of the way in which they have come to exploit different food sources, while living cheek by jowl with their neighbours of different species. There will be a fringe of black-headed gulls along the tideline, fishing and roosting herons, cormorants on the Harbour Authority pontoons, possibly terns fishing or perching on the yacht masts. There may be the best part of a hundred crows working the mud but the main interest will be in the wading shore-birds.

The waders find food by touch, taste, movement and visual clues. Their bills have a mass of sensory nerve endings. Their prey relates to bill size. Dunlin and other small waders work the top couple of inches, where there are plenty of worms and meaty shells. Redshanks specialise in small shells called *Macoma* but

Redshank in flight. Below, left: Redshank. Centre: Spotted redshank. Right: Greenshank.

The long, down-curved bill of the curlew is unmistakeable.

also take small shrimps. The longer bills of godwits and curlews reach deeper for lugworms and gapers. The birds also choose subtly different surface areas over which to hunt.

In summer many of the birds here are non-breeders, but their numbers are swelled as the months go by with returning parents and their families until the numbers reach a maximum at the turn of the year.

Redshank are common as passage migrants and winter visitors, but their maximum is in August/September, when there may be a hundred or so. They have a preference for tidal pools and the water's edge, chasing food at a brisk walk. Spotted redshanks are regular to Devon, but, sadly, not to the Dart, so far as we know. Greenshanks are regular, sometimes in small parties of up to a dozen. They peak in September/October. Dunlin are here in fair numbers, often at the very edge of the water, with the black-headed gulls. Both black-tailed and bar-tailed godwits show up in small numbers, from singles to ten or so. They are almost curlew-sized but with long, straight bills. Working slowly over the mud, head down, they search busily for worms and shells.

The curlews are everyone's favourite, with their long down-curved bills and lovely liquid cry. Solitary, or in parties of mixed company, they stand out by virtue of their size as the largest of the waders, although their plumage could rudely be called streaky mud-coloured. Strolling over the mud, they pause to probe, then maybe run a few feet to pick up an unwary ragworm. With a beak reach of nearly six inches they have free choice of all the mud creatures, even reaching down to the peppery furrow shell. While they may not quite reach down to the lugworm in its chamber, they can and do catch it by the tail as it reaches up to expel detritus in the worm cast. Cockles and other shellfish are swallowed whole, the indigestible shells subsequently rejected in the form of a pellet. On the upper shore, especially in autumn, they hunt the abundant shore crabs by sight, rather than by touch and taste. There may be a couple of hundred on the mud here, congregating after the inland breeding season, although there are always some non-breeders throughout the year. The peak is August/September.

Above: Lapwing and golden plover. Below: Black-tailed godwit, bar-tailed godwit.

Some lapwings breed elsewhere in Devon, but they are most abundant in autumn and winter on the estuaries. On the Dart there may be a flock of a hundred or two in August/September. The grass fields behind the tidal mud are as important to them as the surface mud for feeding. As with oystercatchers and curlews they often stay behind on the roosting fields long after the receding tide begins to uncover the mud, unlike the smaller waders which don't waste a minute of mud-hunting time. The neatly laid out orchards of **Whitestone Farm**, incidentally, are experimental cider orchards belonging to Whiteways.

Sadly, there are no wintering spoonbills or avocets on the Dart, but we live in hope. Neither are there any wintering geese. No *Zostera* beds, so no brent geese and precious few wigeon. In fact, surprisingly few wildfowl use this estuary. Perhaps a couple of hundred mallard, a handful of wigeon and teal, a few pairs of mute swans and no geese at all. There is a shortage of

In flight: Three mallards, two teal and a wigeon. In the water, left and centre: Drake and duck mallard. Above and right: Drake and duck teal. Ashore: Drake and duck wigeon.

open foreshore, the tidal reaches are generally too narrow and deepset to support the sort of vegetation that suits wildfowl.

Shelducks do fairly well, with probably a dozen pairs breeding successfully most years, but they tend to inhabit reaches high up, although both Old Mill and Dittisham Mill Creeks harbour a few breeding pairs and provide a courting area in winter and early spring.

Sedge warbler

IV

THE UPPER REACHES

At the top end of Long Stream the banks close in and the channels merge to take boats over to the west side, under the trees of **Kirkham Copse.** Along the foreshore here there are usually several tree trunks and branches cast ashore and gently rotting. There may be ducks, and it is a likely area for kingfishers, perching close above the waterline. A surprising number of land birds find pickings on the foreshore, so you may also see woodpigeons, robins and thrushes taking advantage of the small stuff; sandhoppers and worms abound.

At the entrance to **Bow Creek** there are quite likely to be a few waders and this is one of the favoured places for shelducks. In the early part of the season, until the end of June, there may be several dozen of them sporting themselves in the waterside fields and, of course, they are very easy to spot. Large and goose-like, they have a striking chestnut band round their chests, dark green head and red bill, all carried on a white body. When the tidal mudbanks are uncovered boats pass very close to their preferred feeding grounds. In April and May the off-duty birds will be working the mud solo but, from the first week in June, when most clutches hatch, the family parties will be trailing over the mud in well-defined groups. At this time of the year the estuary is a fairly quiet place from the birdwatcher's point of view, because the tidal nature of the habitat means that very few birds breed here. Mute swans may build their nests on the saltings, a risky undertaking, since the nests and eggs are usually swept away by spring tides. But at this time the majority of estuary birds are thousands of miles away in the high Arctic and in Scandinavia so it is specially good to have the company of the shelducks, which do stay to breed. They will have been courting

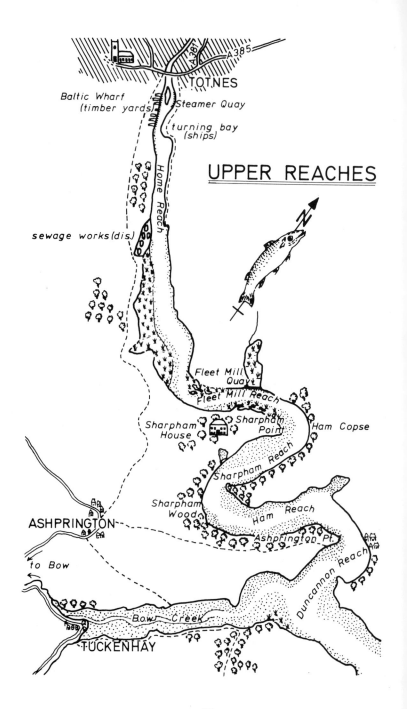

UPPER REACHES

Baltic Wharf
(timber yards)

TOTNES

Steamer Quay

turning bay
(ships)

Home Reach

sewage works (dis.)

Fleet Mill
Quay

Fleet Mill Reach

Sharpham
House

Sharpham
Point

Ham Copse

Sharpham Reach

ASHPRINGTON

Sharpham
Wood

Ham Reach

Ashprington Pt.

to Bow

Duncannon Reach

Bow Creek

TUCKENHAY

46

noisily since the turn of the year; anything up to a dozen birds promenading on the mud and taking part in highly formalised dancing parties. Long before spring they have chosen a nesting place, perhaps underground in a rabbit burrow, or hidden in the depths of a bramble bush above the marsh and, while one bird sits tight on the dozen eggs, the other will stand sentinel out on the saltings or on the fields nearby.

When the ducklings hatch, after thirty days of incubation, they must go down to the mudflats where they find their food. At twenty-four hours of age they are led from the burrow by their parents, across fields, ditches, hedges, roads and all—then across the saltings to gain the safety of the mud. Inevitably, on the way, some ducklings fall prey to marauding foxes and crows. Once on the mud, the duck introduces them to the delights of ragworms and shellfish, while the drake stands guard. Gulls and crows are always ready to take advantage of the unwary duckling which strays too far from the safety of the family circle and, by the time the ducklings are a week or two old, the brood is usually reduced to half a dozen or less. Shelducks have a very

Shelducks. Left: Duck. Right: Drake

loose family bond. Week-old ducklings will readily join the nearest brood or crêche when they are alarmed and, by the time they are three weeks old, they are almost independent. From now on they will mix freely with the ducklings of other families, forming a crêche supervised by just one pair of adults. Whether these playschool supervisors are self-appointed, chosen, or just landed with the job by virtue of being the last pair to hatch ducklings, is unclear. Certainly, by the time ducklings are a month old, their parents are beginning to leave the home estuary to fly away on a moult migration, perhaps to Bridgewater Bay. They join thousands of others to find safety in numbers during this vulnerable period, when they are confined by their flightless state to sandbank and sea, while they moult and grow new flight feathers. In the early winter they make a leisurely way back to the Dart.

In the first part of June you may see half-a-dozen family parties of shelducks between Bow Creek and Totnes but, by the middle of July, there is hardly an adult to be seen, and the fast-growing ducklings keep themselves to themselves. Fortunately, by this time there are plenty of other things to look for.

If you have the chance to penetrate the mile or so up Bow Creek to **Tuckenhay** it is well worth the effort. Tuckenhay itself is a quiet enough place today, but it was once a hive of industrial activity, with paper and corn mills and a gasworks which introduced the pleasures of gaslight to this remote village in the same year in which it was introduced to London, 1806. Bow Creek is served by the rivers Harbourne and Wash, which jointly produce enough water to float a swan or two when the tide is out. Following the main ship channel to Totnes we are in deeper water, though even here the pleasure boats are severely restricted and cannot operate on these head waters less than an hour and a half either side of low water.

With Bow Creek behind us we enter **Duncannon Reach.** The river narrows abruptly, with a splendidly open field slope (good for oystercatchers and curlews) on one side leading gently down to **Ashprington Point.** On the starboard hand, oak-fringed fields lead to the hamlet of **Duncannon**. At one time the steamers used to land passengers here for Stoke Gabriel, which lies just the other side of the hill, and today the Stoke Gabriel men still come here for the salmon fishing.

The salmon season runs from 16 March to 16 August. Eighteen licences allow the fishermen to work every day except between 6 a.m. on Saturday to 6 a.m. Monday. They may work from first light to last, varying the beaches from which they

Duncannon Reach.

shoot their seine nets according to the tides. At neaps they stick
to the main waterway, while springs allow them to penetrate
more of Bow Creek. The catch varies from year to year but, for
instance, one year's haul, as reported in the South West Water
Authority's Annual Fisheries Report, was 748 salmon and 250
sea trout, adding up to 8,550 lbs weight of fish. The individuals
vary from, say, six to twelve pounds in weight. The Dart
compares well with other West Country estuaries for salmon
numbers, and, inevitably, poaching is something of a problem.
If you are daring enough to go boating on the river at night
there is a real possibility of getting fouled in illegal gill-nets. The
poachers will certainly be using boats which show no navigation
lights.

The Atlantic salmon is a passage migrant here. Born higher
up the river, the young fish live their first years in the fresh
water, before migrating down to the open sea and the plankton-
rich waters of the northern North Atlantic. Most of their adult
life is spent at sea, growing fat; but they return to their native
rivers to spawn. In a summer of drought, they may congregate in
the estuaries in large numbers, waiting for the rainfall which
provides them with enough fresh water to smell their way up the
rivers. This is the time when they may be taken in seine nets and,
thereby, denied the chance to spawn or fertilise. Never miss a
chance to join the netsmen at their work and, perhaps, see one
of these splendid fish. Look carefully at its body and, if it is

Leaping salmon and its sea-louse.

fresh-run, there may be a number of sea-lice clinging to it. These parasites do not survive long in fresh water, so the estuary is the most likely place for you to see them. Only a centimetre or so long, they have a hollow flattened body which acts as a suction disc, pressing against the fish skin. Two prehensile claws dig into the flesh and grip hard.

Eels are common in these waters, although their life-history is almost the mirror-image of that of the salmon. They spend some time here during their youthful journey upstream from the Atlantic spawning grounds, then in due course make their last, down-stream journey in the silver livery of spawning. They are taken in fair numbers by the cormorants. Choosing a likely area, the bird does a jack-knife dive into the muddy water and searches the bottom using every sense but sight, to emerge with a wriggling eel that may be as long as himself. The struggle to swallow it may be dramatic and prolonged. Having achieved a full belly, the cormorant has a pressing need to rest and recuperate. The spit off Ashprington Point is a favourite place for this activity. There may well be a dozen of these primitive-looking snake-birds basking on a sunny day at this unfrequented spot.

Cormorants are totally at home in and under the water, but they waddle clumsily as soon as they come ashore, so they avoid walking any distance. Struggling a few feet to join their mates, or maybe a group of oystercatchers, they shake the surface water off themselves like a dog, then face into the wind and spread their wings out to dry. After a few minutes of this decorative inactivity, they preen vigorously, then stand about for anything up to several hours. This roosting may well be interspersed with a fishing trip or two. They prefer to dive in shoal water, even as shallow as a foot or so. Less than half a minute is often enough for them to find prey, but they are able to stay down well over a minute. Normally they bring their catch to the surface to swallow it, head first, but if it is large or recalcitrant they may bring it ashore to deal with it. They eat something like two pounds of fish a day. Sedentary birds, with slow, labouring flight, they spend a good deal of time at rest, and may live their whole lives within a watery stretch of, say, twenty miles.

In the breeding season they roost on their off-shore breeding station at the Mewstone but, for the rest of the year, they stay in the shelter of the estuary waters, roosting at night in trees. The major roost is after we have passed Ashprington Point. **Sharpham Wood** rises steeply on the left of **Ham Reach.** The roosting cormorants (and there may well be some there at any

Cormorants preening and wing-drying at Ashprington Point.

(Tony Soper)

At the cormorant roost. The juveniles have white shirt-fronts.

time of the day as well as at night) are in a tall sycamore just
inshore of the red port hand buoy marked 'Sharpham S'. It is
easy enough to spot the tree, if not the birds, because it is
liberally sprinkled with their white droppings. A little further
on, still on the port hand, there is another, less favoured, roost
in an oak just before the starboard hand black-and-white pole
with a green topmark.

Sharpham Wood was the home of a heronry, famous since the
Middle Ages, but in 1961 there was a great deal of felling which
unfortunately disturbed them. All may be well in the long run
as, in the spring of 1981, one pair returned close by to breed
successfully and possibly be the forerunners of a heronry
revival.

A sharp turn past Sharpham boathouse opens **Sharpham
Reach.** The deep water channel follows the east side. **Sharpham
House** itself stands on a hill top, remote and cool, as the river
sweeps round its promontory in a half-circle. Georgian, it was
built between 1770 and 1825 for a naval captain whose money
came from a Spanish prize. The architect was Sir Robert

Cormorant battling with an eel. Notice how low they float in the water.

Taylor. The gardens may have been designed, but were more likely influenced, by Capability Brown. If you take care not to blink an eyelid you may glimpse between the trees a Henry Moore bronze female figure and a Barbara Hepworth 'Persephone' on the terrace as you round Sharpham Point.

The pleasure-boat skippers may mislead you with talk about Sharpham being a 'calendar house' with 365 windows etc etc, but you will be more usefully employed looking for birds. Do not cut the corner as you pass a port hand buoy but keep well over to the steep-to starboard side into **Fleet Mill Reach.** Ham Copse, with its hanging oak wood and steep banks, is on your right. These wooded gorges have led people, starting with Queen Victoria, to describe the Dart as the 'English Rhine', though the description better fits the upper reaches of the Tamar Estuary. Their main claim to a naturalist's attention is that for the past ten years or so this has been a rallying point for passage ospreys.

Ospreys occur every autumn in very small numbers on the West Country estuaries, on the way from their Scottish or Scandinavian breeding lakes to winter quarters in North Africa

Top: Buzzard and (below it) osprey in flight. Osprey at typical perch, a dead branch.

and along the Mediterranean coast of Spain and southern Portugal. But our Dart osprey has been a most dependable regular, arriving in mid-August and leaving in mid-September, although some years it stays later (for instance, I saw it on 7 October in 1981). On at least one (10 Sept 1976) and possibly two (6 Aug 1975) occasions two have been seen. The August record was given to me by a tripper-boat skipper who had seen 'two buzzards splashing into the water'. On one unforgettable occasion we saw the osprey perched on a dead branch by the waterside at **Sharpham Point.** It took off lazily and dropped heavily into the coarse grass of a field. We heard its shrill mewing call, with a distinct drop in pitch at the end. A couple of hours later, as we were sailing downstream, we saw the bird flying from Stoke Gabriel across to Bow Creek with a two-pound fish held torpedo fashion in its spiney feet. Most often we have seen them perching on the bare branches of dead or partly-dead trees, often well back from the water's edge.

The passage ospreys may be seen anywhere from Waddeton up to Sharpham, but the area between Duncannon and Sharpham has given us the most sightings. Be careful not to confuse them with the common buzzards which may often be surprisingly white. The ospreys have the bold black stripe through the eye on a more-or-less white head. Their small heads seem sunk back behind the well 'bowed' wings with their black carpal patches in flight, and, of course, they display great interest in the water. In our experience they are pleasantly unmoved by passing boats. Ospreys used at one time to breed on Lundy and the cliffs of North Devon and, in the 18th century, at Beer in East Devon. Nowadays, however, all records are of passage migrants.

Entering **Fleet Mill Reach** there is a modest patch of saltings and mud on the Sharpham side, where the occasional curlew and a few gulls may be feeding, as well as several parties of shelducks in season. On the other side Fleet Mill Creek has a man-made barrage across its entrance, retaining a useful lake of fresh water and *Phragmites* beds. In these reed-beds sedge warblers breed in summer and, since 1967, there have been records of breeding reed warblers, which are on the increase in Devon. Arriving at the end of April, both sedge and reed warblers may easily be heard at all times of the day and night, but much less easily seen. Reed buntings are resident and fairly common.

Lying against the sea-wall is the rusting hulk of 'Kingswear Castle', one of the steam paddlers which worked the Dart-mouth-Totnes pleasure service for the sadly defunct River Dart

In the reeds: Cock (top) and hen reed bunting. On the shore: Common sandpiper. In the water: Little grebes.

Steamboat Company. Taken out of service in 1924 she served as a hospital ship until abandoned in the thirties.

In this reach you may well see the barge 'Bilsdale' securely anchored 'all-fours' and dredging sand from the bottom. She can pick up a full load of 180 tons in a working day, taking it back to her home wharf at Totnes. Anywhere in these head waters you may see small groups of little grebes (dabchicks) from about mid-September through to March, although they do sometimes breed here. Generally speaking there is a shortage in Devon of slow-running rivers and tranquil ponds of the sort which encourage little grebes to nest. In any case they are much less secretive after the breeding season.

Common sandpipers are indeed common along the tidal creeks and foreshores from mid-July, becoming most plentiful in autumn. Some of them stay to winter. Their high-pitched whistle, 'kitty-wiper', penetrates even the most powerful diesel engine noises as you cruise the channel. Often you first see them flying close to the water to land at the very edge. Dull brown above and white below, their jerky, bobbing action is unmistakeable, as they search for insects in shallow water or over the mud and stones.

At the upper end of Fleet Mill Reach there is a red port hand post which marks **Forty-foot rock**, a hazard which, not surprisingly, lies just underwater forty feet from the shore. There is a sharp bend in the channel here, and it seems improbable that 1,000 ton coasters may negotiate it, but they do. Dave Griffiths, the Trinity House Pilot for the Dart, regularly guides Danish timber-ships of anything up to 247 feet in length and with a 35 foot beam through these bends on their way to deliver softwood to Totnes. With an average draught of 12 feet he has to work his tides carefully but, if you are lucky, you will see one of the Bres Line vessels thread its way majestically through these winding waters and this bend represents the trickiest turn of the lot.

Now the curves give way to the mile-and-a-half **Home Reach**, narrow and straight and leading directly to Totnes. The four-square sandstone tower of St. Mary's church stands out well in the distance. On the starboard hand is a fringe of saltings which may harbour a few curlews roosting at the top of the 'cliff'. On the port hand and behind a retaining wall, is an extensive area of brackish lagoons, **Sharpham Barton Marsh**. More sedge warblers inhabit the reed-beds here, and there may well be a green sandpiper about. These fresh-water marshes, which are only slightly salted by the estuary waters, make an ideal habitat

Sharpham Barton Marsh and the Home Reach leading to Totnes.

(Tony Soper)

for this species. Larger than the common sandpiper they have darker backs, but are best identified in flight, when they seem almost black above, with a white rump and dark end to the tail. They are regular passage migrants here, usually in August, though it is possible the odd one stays for the winter.

The now-disused sewage treatment tanks which form the upper end of this marsh provide a great attraction for black-headed gulls. They are usually well established here, sitting sociably on the tops of the fence-posts. As the pleasure-boats pass be sure to enjoy the skill with which they exploit the worms and titbits disturbed by the passing wash. Most of these gulls will be in their winter colours, of course, with white heads and dark ear-patches instead of the chocolate heads of breeding plumage. However, they still sport the slender red bill and red legs which make them such attractive little gulls. Buzzards may well be wheeling over the open fields on either side of this reach. A small sycamore wood on the west side now leads us to **Baltic Wharf**, the timber terminus for the coasters. Fully loaded, they may bring 1700 cubic metres of softwood to unload onto the quay. The timber comes mainly from Finland, but also Russia, Sweden and Poland, and it is destined for the building trade. In the past, there have also been cargoes of chipboard from Ireland and even thatching reed from Holland. The ships are turned for the downstream journey with the help of the dredged turning bay on the opposite side of the river. Just upstream of the timber wharf is the base for the sand-dredger 'Bilsdale' and, if she is not lying alongside, you will at least see the piles of building sand she has claimed from the river bed.

Now we approach the pleasant and ancient town of **Totnes.** If you saw no mallard ducks lower down in the estuary you will certainly see some now, but these will be the familiar tame ducks of city parks, as different from the wild and shy winter visitors as chalk from cheese. If you want to enjoy their company, walk round to **Vire Island** for a picnic. To do this you must cross over a late fifteenth century bridge over the Dart and only a few hundred yards from the weir which marks the highest point penetrated by salt water. Once it may have been possible to go as high as Dartington on a tide but now these headwaters, fished by anglers and cormorants, are navigated only by salmon and canoeists.

Totnes is a lovely place, built on the side of a steep hill, and much of the wall which enclosed the twelfth century town is still standing, to say nothing of the Castle, with its Norman earthworks. In Elizabethan times it was a prosperous wool port and it retains a civilised charm, something of a cultured atmosphere and good shops. In 1724 Daniel Defoe said of it that it was inhabited by 'more gentlemen than tradesmen' and that may well still be true!

APPENDIX

Pleasure boat services

1. Services from Dartmouth to Totnes, return, running from Easter to the end of October:
    Red Cruisers (G.H. Ridalls & Sons) Dartmouth 2109. Tickets from kiosks on the North and South Embankments.

    River Link (Dart Pleasure Craft) Dartmouth 3145 and Totnes 862735. Tickets from kiosks on the North and South Embankments.

2. Service from Dartmouth to Dittisham:
    River Dart Services Dartmouth 2573. From the South Embankment to the Ferry Pontoon, Dittisham. Easter to beginning of October.

3. Service from Dartmouth (South Embankment) to Dartmouth Castle:
    Summer months, shuttle service, 'Castle Ferry' from steps opposite Old Post Office.

4. Services also run daily in the season from Torquay, Paignton and Brixham by way of Torbay, Berry Head and the coast to Dartmouth, Dittisham and Totnes (destination depends on tide times).

5. Self-drive hire boats:
    from the kiosks at Double Steps, North Embankment, Dartmouth. Or John or Brian Ridalls, of the Red Cruisers kiosks, may fix you up with 'Sturdy', an ex-pilot launch which is ideal for exploring the Dart.

6. Wildlife cruises:
    Programme from Tony Soper, Gersbon Point, Kingsbridge, Devon TQ7 3BA.

Yacht Clubs

Royal Dart Yacht Club: Kingswear 272
Dartmouth Yacht Club: Dartmouth 2305
Dittisham Sailing Club: no premises
Totnes Boating Club: Totnes

Chandlers

The Bosun's Locker, 24 Lower Street, Dartmouth (2595)
Coopers Sailing and Boating Centre, Totnes (862255)
Dartmouth Chandlers (Hayward Marine), 24 Foss Street,
    Dartmouth (3900)
Dartmouth Boating Centre, South Embankment,
    Dartmouth (2125)

Yards

Philip & Son Ltd., Noss Works, Dartmouth
Creekside Boatyard, Old Mill Creek, Dartmouth
Dartmouth Yacht Services, Mayor's Avenue

Harbour Authority

The Dart Harbour and Navigation Authority, the Old
Post Office, South Embankment, Dartmouth (2337) publishes a
useful (and free) booklet of pilotage notes and small craft
facilities for the harbour and the Dart.

The Imray yachting chart for the River Dart is Y47.

Local Societies

The principal ornithological society for the county is the
Devon Birdwatching and Preservation Society (Hon. member-
ship secretary: Mrs. H.A. Woodland, Blacksmith's Cottage,
West Raddon, Shobrooke, Crediton. Hon. Recorder: P.W.
Ellicott, Clitters, Trusham, Newton Abbot, TQ13 0LX).

The principal conservation society for the county is the
Devon Trust for Nature Conservation, 75 Queen Street, Exeter.

Dartmouth and Kingswear Society. Information from the
Harbour Bookshop, Fairfax Place, Dartmouth TQ6 9AE, which
also has a wide range of natural history and nautical books.

INDEX

References to line drawings and photographs are in italics.

63